Accla

"As beautifully forn
Backwards Men' inspires deep feeling and introspection. Kocsis' stunning prose probes the tenderest parts of her heart, allowing the reader to touch those spots in themselves. Her words weave an emotional tapestry bravely hanging in the corridor of our collective soul, and we are all the better for it. These words go beyond cognition; they fill the mind's eye with images and the heart-mind with transformative emotion. I have no doubt this book will inspire all who read it to dive inward, cuddle up with their shadow, and move forward with a loving, healed heart."

Melissa M. Monroe, Ph.D., L.Ac is a doctor of
traditional classical Chinese medicine, the author of the book "Mom's Search for Meaning: Grief and Growth after Child Loss," and host of the podcast, "This Club Suuucks: Grief Support for Parents After the Lasagnas are Long Gone."

"Gorgeous, lyrical, and moving, 'Keeper of Backwards Men' is the empowering read your heart needs. Ms. Kocsis is a master at not simply tugging at our hearts; she breaks hers, and ours, open. A powerful must-read gift to ourselves."

Rachel Thompson, author of the award Winning Broken series, RachelintheOC.com

"In 'Keeper of Backwards Men' Vennie Kocsis offers meditations, marvels, and mysteries. Her lyrical and meaningful descriptions create a space for deep introspection. She reminds us we move to our rhythms and needs in our own time. *'Time is the dance of chance. This time I understand that you need time, and this time I may let time carry me on.'* An absolute delight of words cleansing life's struggles."

Dr. J. | Donna Jennings, Ph.D. Editor. Educator. Author. "Purple Sex and Love Beyond Your Dreams: A Women's Guided Journal to Explore Your Sexual Self." drjauthor.com

A Note from the Editor

Dear Readers,

It is with great pleasure and excitement that I present to you this extraordinary collection of writing. As the editor, I have had the privilege of immersing myself in the profound and enchanting words that adorn the pages of this book. Each poem is a delicate masterpiece, carefully crafted by a talented and imaginative writer who has poured her heart and soul into her work.

Vennie Kocsis uses verse to fearlessly explore the depths of human existence, touching upon themes of love, loss, hope, and the myriad complexities of life. Her words have the power to transport you to ethereal landscapes, evoke forgotten memories, and ignite sparks of introspection.

May these pages be a sanctuary where your imagination takes flight, your emotions find resonance, and your spirit finds solace. May the enchantment of the expressions be your constant companion, inspiring you to embrace the beauty and wonder of the world.

With warmest regards,

Lisa LaMarr, Editor

Keeper of Backwards Men

by

VENNIE KOCSIS

All rights reserved. No part of this book may be reproduced, scanned, or distributed in any printed or electronic form without permission. Please do not participate in or encourage piracy of copyrighted materials in violation of the author's rights. Purchase only authorized editions.

According to copyright law, specifically the first sale doctrine, it is illegal to resell eBooks because eBooks are not physical goods. This book may not be reproduced in any form, digital, media, print or any other form, under penalty of violation of copyright law.

For information, address:

Vennie Kocsis
2661 North Pearl St. #258
Tacoma, WA 98407

ISBN: 9798386724955

Cover and Art © 2023 Vennie Kocsis

DBV Publishing

All rights reserved.

Editor: Lisa LaMarr

Dedications

My sons, your resiliency, fight for change, and passion for this life beyond all adverse experiences is humbling. You have taught me the meaning of redemption and acceptance. You are kings. You will always be the anchors for my heart.

My sweet grandchildren may these words live long into your future generations and remind you of the richness in your DNA. You are sacred beyond all measures.

From the Author

Each piece in this book has been curated from thirty years of unpublished writing. May these words serve your emotional processing and way forward. I hope you remember to let go of that which has served its purpose and accept your new without fear.

You are never alone, and you matter. In moments of struggle, sitting in stillness or should your intuition call, pick up this book, choose a page, and let the words resonate.

CONTENTS

1 Kinesis   11
2 Nascent   55
3 Omnipotent   95
4 Womanhood   133
5 Inherent   169
6 Numinous   189
7 Guardian   217

1. KINESIS

ki·ne·sis
/kəˈnēsis/
noun
movement; motion.

Vennie Kocsis

Let us get started with introspection, possibilities, and realms that are limitless. If you wish to travel through space and morph into portals you gotta open the inside and let yourself merge to take that ride.

Grave digger, you must sweat and dig up the bones.

Traverse the mire and dive into your depth. Just wait until you discover the beauty of your existence. It will be magnificent.

Keeper of Backwards Men

I want to ride time, grasp onto her reins, skimming over her wave as she shows me the journey I tried to manipulate.

Time wears no watch, sounds neither bells nor the tick-tock of a metal clock. No numeric measure exists to cage her.

She speaks in whispers, situations, and the serenity of the leaves.

Time is the dance of chance. This time I understand that you need time, and this time I may let time carry me on.

It is in the breeze, those whispers. I am a messenger.
I speak about light lightly. I am in his zone where
elevated laughter sets the undertone of individual life
form.

Gone are the headlights. Stuck wild gaze creature,
into the bliss I walk.

                Geometric dimension.

Soul life and love life.

Keeper of Backwards Men

Wandering, I am not lost. I stride without hesitation into the waiting tide, lover of peaceful pacing, gathering stones,

        painting star shine,

                breathing.

The dutiful shape shifter becoming siren and sand, I fluidly move between water and land.

Riding on clouds, dragons silently drift, as storms turn them into butterflies propelled by truth.

It was so calm, the way we floated, all hoping and open, our raft wide with expanse.

We had a purpose.

We took a chance.

Intuition rose slowly and even when my gut said, "go, please!" I did not stand to gather my possessions.

The storm hit the day I found myself hand to throat against walls. I would call the name of gods no one ever knew.

The calm before that storm was eerie and too morbid for the soul. It held the whisper of a rage that I could not interpret or escape.

I watch that storm dissipate through the healing and dealing with heavy days. I release the desperate grey and step gingerly away from yesterday.

Keeper of Backwards Men

You see, every moment I fall you leave, and I am here, bandaging new wounds, layering on salve to make the pain dispel.

You have a story for every empty spot. I sit with black abysses in mason jars, overlooked, a puppeteer with the strings cut. You cannot understand the intricacy of these caves. Your legs cannot withstand the waves. You don't know yet, but I will run away.

Even when you were standing right next to me, the distance and energy said you were a million miles away.

You were parched for my words, as if they were the last drop of water that you would ever consume, comforting you during solitary nights.

Our own inflated senses of ego served as a mask. We never considered ourselves good enough.

Your emotions were shredded into so many pieces that they melted into the linings of your heart and hardened.

You have retreated into silence. How do we shape something that has been turned into stone?

Keeper of Backwards Men

The face grins with focused eyes, working to balance the churning inside. It is how the wounded have survived walking the human plank, life after life.

It is the overwhelming influx of matter from the incessant chatter of surroundings, so the body searches constantly for grounding.

That is what exists behind the smile lines, everything that winds and rewinds into a sorted mass of entangled matter making the brain scatter.

In the end what really matters is that you gather the tattered pieces, weaving the mania into mosaics, and having the final say in it.

Vennie Kocsis

I have become a mother to myself, nights where the weeping girl within me soaked pillows with the pain of pasts.

"It doesn't last, my dear," she says softly. "one day it all fades away."

Reversing hours is risky, examining each loss, and learning to grieve the drowning messages of Pentecost.

I stand back and survey.

I am both resigned and dismayed.

Keeper of Backwards Men

Seeing does not always happen in the eyes. It lives in the fingertips, the senses, the smells and sounds that surround my skin. I dive inside the layers, following the trails to the hidden spaces, the places where the knowledge hides inside.

Into the dense matter I dive, fearlessly igniting my shine.

Vennie Kocsis

I send messages through clouds, open curtains to catch your scent, stand silent in the wind to hear your voice again.

Refusal makes smiles go missing. They leave the damaged gasping for the truth, but it all got buried with you.

Keeper of Backwards Men

You could not know the affect unless you lived it.

You could not know the loss unless you have given it.

There is water, and icebergs, waiting to reserve my soul until I learn to stop leaving it in unreceptive places.

Vennie Kocsis

I left half a life on the frozen ground of Delta Junction, Alaska, buried beneath a wooden paddle and stripped skin.

I dragged the remnants across the tundra, down the open range until my knees bled, begging for freedom; a soul murdered, wandering, left only a scream.

I sought forgiveness on the soaked mattresses of strangers, watching the eyes of men, glistening like arrows shot into the soft fur of little lambs standing robotic, cold, and hollow.

Flayed open like zippers torn on skirts, the whole of humanity rushed through me; rivers of sorrow, so thick, my heart wept repeatedly.

Sequestered I become my own domain. I travel the hallways of my mind, bringing illumination into the unexplored spaces.

To be a chosen one is not special. It is a journey through the caverns of human hell.

Vennie Kocsis

The box awaits my arrival; its hinges creaking,
practicing the closing as I gather stones, heart shaped,
into my skirt, the ghosts of little girls lost in the fields.

The sun sets black, dripping orange like all hallowed
eves. I swallow back realizations that self-absorption
is a disease erasing the face of empathy running rabid
through the brain stems of the masses.

Keeper of Backwards Men

Sometimes the wind blows in directions uncharted, small summer storms. I sit motionless in the grass, and I listen.

Sometimes the wind blows lessons through scattering seeds inside the ruins left behind. Gardens spring up rich with fruit and filled with the scent of what I once loved about you.

Sometimes the wind blows and I leap a cloud into the distant unknown.

Sometimes the wind blows, and I am the only one who knows.

Vennie Kocsis

It is a scent that lingers and stings like rain, like the first refrain of violins when the pain begins.

It is a dance of tangos and melancholy tears for the master of ceremonies. I am just a joker walking the wire.

I am smelling wood coals pressed in my face while your fingertips press hollow bullets into my rib cage.

Keeper of Backwards Men

Where do I go when I float? Away from the frayed tentacles of memories and torn ligaments, strained from twisting, and turning.

"Child," they said, "this hurts me more than it hurts you."

They are killers of dreams, soul murderers, and sheep herders.

There is a monumental descension, sociopathy, human feet

> Shuffling...

> > Shuffling...

away from empathy.

Predatory energy is disrupting our synergy.

Humans long so deeply for the things that keep them weeping.

Beaten down, blue in the soul, I stand by watching chemical clouds unfold.

Keeper of Backwards Men

It was not until I learned to float that life became liquid. It was not until I opened my eyes that I saw how far I had drifted. I have started swimming.

Vennie Kocsis

The rushed filter of the day has left you breathless. Your mind races with thoughts, wonder and worry.

Where to find peace amid chaos?

Close your eyes. Deliver yourself into yourself. See. Feel. Become private. Escape time by letting it cease to matter.

Inside the turning and twisting is pure honesty. In the heart of the swirling is your laughter. In the center of this Universe is your BE-ing, all knowing and all accepting of you.

Allow you to fall in love with your hues.

Keeper of Backwards Men

My gold is woven in possibilities and endless patterns of emerging change. Sunsets have no end nor do sunrises begin. It is an infinite timelessness merging days into slow minutes.

Everything can change in an instant. Tides turn as I row with the ebbs. This sea is vaster than I can see.

Vennie Kocsis

Oh, the incredible waves of life. I feel like a slinky going up the stairs instead of down. Life is changing – dreams held silent for years suddenly exploding like fireworks, and hold on a minute, can I breathe here?

I suddenly have heart burn; do not want this wheel to spin too fast. I am hunkering down for the winter. It is right around the corner after this heat wave passes.

Change whirls all around me. It is pressing like a child's face against a glass, distorted, not yet in view.

I should start naming my hurricanes, so the searchers can identify the remains.

Keeper of Backwards Men

Not everything on this terrain is born and grown the same. Soft, the colors speak in languages, singing. The layers fade. Nothing matters, not the tatters of aftermath or the worn-out disasters.

I curl up inside the hoping like plasma and jasmine meringue in the vortex.

Vennie Kocsis

I danced beneath the moon's eye at nightfall, distant echoes of wolves singing, each paying reverence to their goddess orb, freed spirits of the dark haunting my circle.

Grace became my soul's fight, and so it was that high above the ocean's edge sweeping in the tide I broke the chains.

Jaunting patterns of sand swallowed my footprints. Kites lay torn from commanding wind screams leaving tracks and water streams.

No mystical distractions, I hovered above the foaming sea and examined the reflection of me.

Keeper of Backwards Men

We create our own shell, enter it and sometimes our ethereal strings connect. Just like children we talk through invisible cans.

Left behind. Standing to the side. We are the shadow lurkers. The odd ones out.

Vennie Kocsis

I am an integrated introvert immersed in the colors keeping my sanity intact.

Keeper of Backwards Men

The sand is closing in on me, deepened by my step, drawing me to my knees. I struggle toward the edge, further away than the moon.

I want to talk to the Universe and ask it why people are shaped so differently, down in the DNA.

Vennie Kocsis

You do not know how deep it goes; no idea the reckoning, like a waking storm that will engulf you with raging waves.

I see inside the patterns people try to hide. It is amazing how breath is like truth serum.

Mouth parched. Lips dry, grasping for spit as you lie.

Keeper of Backwards Men

I watched you shyly the day I slept and woke to the sound of your absence.

I traveled my healing silently with nights of secluded concern. I chose to grow and learn. I increased my expectation and realization of my own knowing, sections of my pride rapidly dethroning.

Molding creation, hands unclench with feeling my soul bloomed in healing.

Music in my ear, feet moving distant chants, I expelled the angered rants.

Eyes besotted with tears, washing dust to see, I am not afraid to bleed.

Speaking to my peace, I night travel in dreams.

Never have I seen someone so incapable of loving themselves; stuck in a rut for so long. It is like snooping around into a past life. To my surprise, I do not care much either way how things turn out right now. My hallways became completely devoid when I opened all the doors.

The potentially lethal components of myself, which I have learned to control, struggled against their restraints. There is no less hurt or regret than there was before. I have just developed the ability to manage the swells.

Keeper of Backwards Men

Tired. Morose. Flat. This feels like an aftermath of the rubble from a space shuttle I was never meant to depart from.

Vennie Kocsis

Outside of this history, the flower fields waved. I ran through them, letting it all dissipate.

What would the handlers say?

"She escaped. She flew away. She did not cave."

Keeper of Backwards Men

Surveying the mind map, I find a sense of calm and serenity. My core belongs to no one else, and no amount of judgment, criticism, misunderstanding, or uncertainty can coax me away from the one and only parcel of land that is solely in my possession.

I drift off to a restful slumber buoyed by the expectation that one will come into existence, one who is aware, one who will look at me and, without using words, convey comprehension.

Vennie Kocsis

I am sand. I drift on breezes. I am swirling scent, colorful frequencies. I am raindrops on faces that cannot cry. Their hearts have gone cold from too many nights of feeling it break, so the ache left them dry with the inability to cry.

I weep on their behalf. Splayed open, I enact my vulnerability without shame, rejecting blame. It blasts through my ear and into invisibility.

I am a ghost disappearing from lingering, pointing fingers.

Keeper of Backwards Men

Avoid the human who will try to convince you that you should feel fear. Maintain a close connection with the human beings who care about both you and the Earth. Encourage one another's spirits and do whatever it takes to grow your love for each other.

You can collectively move the planet forward through individual healing. The key to unlocking your heart is silence—both within you and around you.

Investigate your surroundings. If you find that your mind is muddled, face yourself. Accept the things that need to be fixed. Then dive into the thick of it.

Vennie Kocsis

You can bang the bricks till your head feels thick, until the blood blinds your eyes.

Still, no great journey exists save the places you will go when you choose to travel your own genomes.

We fly so high into the water sky dimensions. Me, her the daughter; she my mother, we are molecules and star dust,

    formed and unformed.

I close my eyes tightly to take in all the sights where colors are felt,

    My spirit held in reverence.

I breathe in blue and exhale purple to feel you. Heal the tears, beautiful.

    You are free.

To you I am just that girl. To those who know me

    I am the sea.

Wave away the fog, love. Cleanse the veil which has held you back from surpassing the roadblocks you befall. Stand gentle inside the tree leaves and breathe in the breeze.

Take each moment slowly. Rewind into stop motion, so you can splay open the projections which spring from the rejection that ails you.

Keeper of Backwards Men

Send the bell. Bang the gong. Follow along if you dare; should you care to stand in the footsteps of thriving in as many weird ways as possible.

I am gonna be a cliff away from absence by the time they notice I am gone.

We always hung there, you know, in the gray with the Grays. They have so much to say.

Vennie Kocsis

I have gained significant insight into who I am. This host, who carries aspects of me, is thoughtful and strong-willed, kind, and generous, intelligent, and free-spirited.

I continue to work through the process of hurt figuring out how forgiveness fits into the equation since forgiveness does not hold the power to perform miracles or bring healing.

Rather, I choose to heal myself. I move my own feet, creating my way forward.

Forgiveness is for the egomaniac.

Keeper of Backwards Men

When your heart tumbles; rolling off your tongue open, unabashed, uninhibited and it is responded to with disregard and apathy, listen to that.

Vennie Kocsis

2. NASCENT

nas·cent
/ˈnās(ə)nt/
adjective
just coming into existence and beginning
to display signs of future potential.

Vennie Kocsis

There are moments I long to go back in the womb. I am preparing to go back swimming and be reborn once more.

Feeling ancient, millenniums old, my soul contracts, breaking water, becoming ready for arrival.

How long is the gestation of heartache? How often do we die before the soul wakes, spitting healing like an infant into existence?

Keeper of Backwards Men

How does an angel let a sad boy know he is worthy of everything good?

    He is gold.

The road is hollow in the shadows. I cannot see your hand through the fog, and I cannot rescue you.

You see, emotion lingers; makes the minutes go slow so it is best to draft a poem and let it seep out to keep it from echoing.

Vennie Kocsis

I want out of this body, out of this place. I am dried out, wrung like a sponge, and assessing escape routes.

I am a faceless wanderer passing by unknown.

There is expanse and planets inside of me that have yet to be born. I am a color wheel glanced at from distances. There is energy in my existence.

I prepare to find a cave, a tender slice of home where there is no noise, the walls are mindful, the specter respects me, and I cease being a blank screen for a multitude of screams.

I am but a blink in this thing we call life. When I return to stardust, I will sleep a thousand nights.

For now, I trudge the wreckage of a complicated pain to see if I can build the strength to return this way again.

Vennie Kocsis

These little waves crash a bit. Caving in I brace for the hits, wondering how long they will last.

I am on the outskirts looking back.

I pass quickly with thoughts that flounder; do not know if I am so lost that I can never be found.

The sun goes down and my desperation whispers.

I wish for minutes to last longer than this, but we have gone into the luminous, where possibilities live.

Some say it is imagination. I call it reverberation.

Keeper of Backwards Men

I am like a baby; like mysteries; like wild cherries staining lips under sycamore trees, a butterfly wing with fading dust trying to flutter. It is a miracle to be alive. I cherish my smile.

I am the raindrops lonely in the sky when they all run inside to not get soaked, ducking under coats, umbrellas, and such, to avoid my moist touch.

I am the cello string, solitary angel wings folding the misery inside of me. Sweep the chimney clean so the voices can sing ancient melodies.

I am like afternoon when life is lazy, the hazy laughter echoing from the rafters, shimmering disaster frequently sought after, but never captured.

I have purpose. They have regret. I have laughter while they fight loneliness. I'm riding foaming crests while they fight panic urges in the chest.

I will not taunt their harvests when the Fall makes her way home. The moon is waning. I have excuses. Do not blame her. I give it up to being.

One day they will understand that I am a solitary star, invaluable and affected by love misdirected.

Keeper of Backwards Men

Do you know those moments your friends take out pictures shoved in boxes or albums, photos of them as babies in their christening gowns, eating popsicles, wearing bell bottoms with suntanned faces?

I flip through them nonchalantly, smiling, exclaiming how wonderful life must have been.

    I am left wondering

What I looked like at five. If I could smile at seven. If my eyes had already gone flat at four.

Vennie Kocsis

I loved you like water, like the grass, like liquid mercury inside of blown glass.

I loved you like soft snow and meditations, like you are the chosen one.

I loved you inside cages, on rooftops where lilies grow through rock quarries.

I loved you innocently like lambs, openly like rain clouds demanding the sun come out. I loved you.

I loved you like disease accustomed to, like rabid dog bites oozing with foam, because the pain had become my home.

I loved you somewhere in the distance like tart lemons and bitter beer faces.

I loved you, and then I loved another.

I loved another like the same as you, same habits, same stench, same brick walls trapped inside the absence.

I loved another like more tears on baby cheeks more bruises on scraped knees, like open wounds and belly screams on roller coaster rides.

I loved another, and then I loved me.

I loved me like acceptance and purity, wholesomeness, and mistakes, like wistful memories and regrets, like fading sunsets.

Keeper of Backwards Men

I loved me like imperfection and joyful smiles, like yearning and fighting, constantly running to keep from hiding.

I loved me, and now I love them.

I love them like learning, figuring it out and compassion, accepting the aftermath of my actions.

I love them like possibility, like understanding choices, like intent of thought and harsh truth.

I love them, because I loved you, who taught me to love another, until I learned to love me, so I could love them.

I am feral in the wild, a thing not meant to be. This place is foreign, temperamental, and scattered with pieces of planets I could not leave behind.

Keeper of Backwards Men

I am stoic inside tranquility, inhaling the scent, the unspoken smiling to myself of how inconvenient it would be to have to tell them what I know. I go into foreign chasms.

    Fail or succeed entirely.

It is nice to have them, tendrils of love, moments of passion and days of consistency. They pull out the comfortable in me, bringing sanity to calm my crazy.

How it both terrifies me and appeals to my half-moon rising

Vennie Kocsis

I have wondered if words will be enough or if purple ink can carry this much love.

My shoulders bear the weight of passing strangers whose eyes hold a longing so deep even the aliens weep.

Tears are on the mirror. I wipe her face and tell her to remember we have been promised grace.

I am walking past churches where the dead men live, the hungry beg and the tax evaders grift.

I am sparking up torches. I am shaking the runes.

Running into the ashes, I emerge brand new.

Keeper of Backwards Men

I drifted silently on calm waters blacker than the moonless midnight.

That night I became nothingness.

That night my death became my life.

Hardwood floors found me curled in a fetal position crawling back to infancy.

That night my blindness became deaf.

That night my brush painted bitter smile lines on my insides.

Vennie Kocsis

Get up, sister sleep.

Weakened state. She is awake, drowning in her heartache and her own mistakes. Her trust breaks.

I hover in a still gaze as she wanders the maze, alive and afraid. How often has she been betrayed?

Get up, sister sleep.

This shit is deep. While you writhe and weep, the blood thirsty feed. Be alert and take heed.

They come in many forms, with a smile and charm, to treat you wrong and do you harm. Do not fall back into slumber. The loss will rip your soul like thunder, making you stumble and blunder.

Get up, sister sleep.

Keeper of Backwards Men

I need the heartbreak just so I can cry. It is hard being the strong one on my knees while they say,

"See? She is not unbreakable."

I was broken all along. In your haste to shove me onto a pedestal you did not pause to notice.

I sit in the aftermath of tragedy's laughing gas, staring at mirrored walls, hoping a smile will relieve the pain for a while.

I have been conditioned. I am deprogramming.

Ever wonder why we hold so tightly to what destroys us, as if without the pain we won't stay alive?

We sit, reminiscing about what could have been, and wondering why. There is no worse sadness than to love without return, to feel passion not rebounded.

Yet there is something self-reflective about the melancholy angst of absence.

Keeper of Backwards Men

I look back. I activate and hesitate to try retracing again to where it began.

Born of sand and fire I leave the dilapidated hell of the bog mire behind me. I do not look back at that torn track.

It has disappeared into the fog of the past never again to have a heartbeat or reach me.

It will be wiped away with time and overgrown vines becoming forest and new life.

Move in cycles and stay wild, child.

Vennie Kocsis

I have traversed fires that were so intense they melted my bones and skin. Words have been hurled at me from forked tongues, cutting and defining each one of my shortcomings.

I have listened to them.

I have experienced the potency of the poison, sucked it down my throat, and processed the rage it caused. I sat back in feigned indifference, aching on the inside, tears filling my lungs, while maintaining a stone face and a steady, rhythmic breathing pattern for the show.

Words make it clear when I am not being understood.

My nature is convoluted. I am unpredictable. I am hard to understand. I cannot help but wonder if loving me is all that dissimilar to loving an infant whose cries can come sporadically needing to be interpreted and responded to.

It is an ebb and flow to let all the trauma go and dig out the claws. Who do they think they are, making a home inside our photons?

I give up everything that has made me what I am, hybrid human and spawn.

I have the sensation of being detached and suspended. This is not an example of dissociation.

This is an algorithm containing places that are more elevated than earth.

I have legs and I walk with them, but at the same time I do not. What a damn juxtaposition. Emotion is an aspect of the human experience that is the most challenging to exert control over.

Words are like stones carved with eternal feelings. They are preserved within the data and last forever. I can be as raw and naked as I want. It makes no difference in the long run. This experience is a blip.

Keeper of Backwards Men

Deeper into the abyss I drift. I evade the takers, the riders, and hiders. I dodge and weave humans who want more pieces of me. I am patched together with new seed. I need pace for fertilizing and growing.

My heartstrings feel so full of love, these days I let my eyes seep the delight. Humanoids call them tears of joy.

I have morphed into triangulated dimensions, new friendships with beautiful intention. We are here rising.

The waiting is over, love. This is Ascension.

Keeper of Backwards Men

Memories become teardrops and scars. I run my
fingertips over the raised bars, listening to music.
There is no other way than injecting it into the earth,
and the plastic cups which held my birth.

Death returns when it
    burns and
        burns and
            burns.

Regrowing the flowers, my skin is ashen from flames.
I am renamed and reclaimed. Shining laughter into
aftermath, I see deeper than seas.

I never said yes to being a test for trauma-altered
DNA.

Shooting for the moon I stage the craft, going back
through portals. I told you I am immortal.

When this skin becomes hollow will I remember the
aches of this life? Will I look back and understand
why?

Releasing into respite, I daydream of the colored
plasma.

Why are you angry?

Why do you show support for despots and tyrants?

Why do you conceal the reality of who you are from others?

Why do you try to validate who you are with things not a part of you?

When do you plan to figure out who you really are?

When are you going to stop fighting against yourself?

When will you be okay with it all?

She expired in loneliness, the kind that creeps up slowly, meshing itself into all the occasions when she said she was alone but never lonely. Solitude will be where she finds the deepest solace.

Vennie Kocsis

When cells are splitting inside her spine, stretching, and weaving, her guides help her turn back time.

Revealing the stealing of innocence, she is consumed with persistence, focus and dedication to the mission. She excuses her existence away from the zones where she does not feel at home.

Her days are spent determined she will not succumb to distractions of attractions or conversations material, a viral suck hole for her soul.

Duality has almost disappeared. Her visual has risen to an observant height where she hears whispered reminders.

"You did not come here to be human."

Keeper of Backwards Men

I am a face behind words read by strangers, and we find ourselves inside of each other.

We remotely view the caverns through the gaps between the letters and sink into the familiar.

We are the eyes of the ones who have survived, brilliant and alive. We are a hive of honey makers, and way pavers unmentioned.

As the fermented tribe of crypt keepers commits self-genocide, we rise. You can run, but you cannot hide.

I am actualized, and that is a weapon.

I see your existence from multiple viewpoints. Fracture your seventh veil to see with the eyes and not the self.

I rise with confidence. I fly into this cosmic realm where human behaviors are linear to lost children trying to find their way home.

I have traveled through the levels of my own perceptions. I have read the scrolls of my history and the shattering I broke through.

I have emerged to view every intricacy of my existence.

I expanded inside the fluid. The gel was soft between my fingers. I stepped on dimensions like stairs. There will never be a stillness like that on this earth. The voices were the melodic opposites of chaotic.

I did not come here to be understood or even loved.

My footprints are swept away by the wind. This will be left amidst the bitter burn of yearning.

I was always destined to be alone, even inside the crowd.

Vennie Kocsis

I am back there in the gradients under mountains where my kin are. I take the timelapse trip into the tunnels of inner earth bliss.

Drop all insecurities. Authenticity is required. Your every thought and desire are revealed in a blink.

Take the bus up Richardson Highway to a place with a gate and a fence, past the guardhouse, through the portal and into the corridors of immortals.

Come, my daughter, with your soft heart. Let us retrace our steps and enter, open and ready to remember.

Bring your Polaroid to capture the permafrost. I know the layout well. Their eyes are mostly green as they glide gently to the scene. Snap the pictures. Capture the family portrait to record this.

The calm has a resonance in the places humans rarely go. There's timber in the air. If you close your eyes, you could find yourself there.

Keeper of Backwards Men

I have unlocked my mind and dove into worlds beyond this place called Earth. I have returned to the unit of my birth. Do not call me back down. I might drown.

Vennie Kocsis

I have always been an insomniac to the stars. There are wars going on for my existence.

The host is weeping. She is weakened by me. I have been a grown woman since I was three.

Good luck with breaking me.

They took her mind apart, inch by inch, scar by scar, until there were just tiny pieces of a heart.

Then they rebuilt her, and she became us. I became me. We became we.

I could make them grow cold; create a diversion, but they are stern these days, focused and watching. We are always preparing for wars.

Now, I think we will take chances and wish for dancing.

Keeper of Backwards Men

The rain is folding in waves against the eaves. I close my eyes to moments of lull. In the intricate weaving of life, a flow emerges.

Remain steady. Stand ready.

I am swaying on cusps, seeing into futures, and I gloat at the prospects before me. This choice I have been given, to live a life of noticing the smallest things, is the most precious gem I hold.

The minutes crumble like stone as you find out that home can be only in yourself. This world is not for otherkin to be coupled with humans.

In the end the hybrid finds aloneness to be their earth's purpose, and being human becomes more of a struggle, sifting through the rubble of broken energy remnants.

Keeper of Backwards Men

I am thinking of home. I am a universal vagabond with my heart strapped on. Ripped so many ways there is no more lining left for stitches. So, I wrap it in twine, tie a knot inside my chest, a place to tether the sadness.

Be elusive, child. Be gentle, yet wild. Stand inside the layers of life's experiences and perspectives. See the full spectrum of who you are.

Stay awake, child. Do not let the whispers of anyone's influence drift into your ears.

You have the knowing inside. Keep it alive.

Keeper of Backwards Men

Hi twin. You out there? I hear you breathing. I am hunting your scent. Do you sense me? You do.

Where did they take you?

We were split for the study. Who would be less vilified? Did I win, twin?

You hide the angst, something is missing; just don't know what. How confusing.

Vennie Kocsis

3. OMNIPOTENT

om·nip·o·tent
/ämˈnipədənt/
adjective
having unlimited power.
able to do anything.

They say, who do you think you are, being happy.
How dare you laugh in bliss. But you smile anyway.
You choose to love, and soon, they find themselves
joining in until the music of healing creates a
symphony.

If I could marry trees and live inside the branches, I would die a thousand deaths just to have infinite chances.

Vennie Kocsis

Existence. Their shadows are lingering in my footsteps, and I cannot catch a breath for the intensity of their desperate loneliness.

The way humans display other humans so they can feel better inside about the way their loved one died, pomp and circumstance taking precedence in lifelessness.

Save the stone. Make me flame in my last moments. Let me shine and be fire. Then take me to the sea where the waves will bury me.

I will return home to tell them of a dying planet and the few eyes who have not yet lost hope.

Keeper of Backwards Men

You darling soul. Do you know how you can grow; how you can generate your own healing and evolve into yourself?

You are an ever-shifting star cluster. Take the helm and drift into the sky. You dance in the light, and you fly.

Vennie Kocsis

I chiseled my path with the smoothest stone.
Encircled by sun beams I have made it my home.
With just the essentials, my bags are packed lightly.
Trust is not promised. I am preparing to go flying.

Weighing the cost, distracted by pictures, I am
fighting for balance away from the malice.

For now, I will follow. I am ripe for the chore when
you meet me at midnight to settle this score.

Keeper of Backwards Men

Feel your own infinite DNA abilities. Understand other beings who walk upright, down low, in form and as translucence. Embrace and accept your future without distraction from your past.

Close your eyes and fly. Rest a moment inside, in the repose. See with the view of yourself from the skies.

You are sunlight.

Discover your garden. Chip away the hardened shell encasing your hell. Choose to illuminate. Fight your way out. Remove yourself from the huddling masses who have become too passive to fight. See this universe with different eyes.

Stand at the crossroads. Choose the path to release the wrath. With all the colors and golden cobbles, reach the end.

Begin again.

Keeper of Backwards Men

Can you hold while I erase this little piece of time, cuz it is mine. I know I gotta be done with this one, because if not, I will endeavor to fix and mend what is already bent beyond repair.

I am a tunnel of tears, emotions, oceans infested with sharks and pieces of myself. Miles ran, more to go, how could I know that these hurdles could become dividers, making me climb higher?

I am flowing rhyme because there's shit I need to leave behind, and god, man, don't it feel grand? I can take slaps, all the jaded epitaphs about perfection and dedication, cuz right here; all I am hearing in my ear is frustration. But that's life, right, a series of seasoned fights?

At this pace I should be a heavyweight.

Wait with restraint. Only in silence you can hear your own voice, and you will finally realize what your songs sound like.

Keeper of Backwards Men

I am soul. I am spirit. I am the bird in the trees. I am music when you hear it. I am prayers on their knees. I am the voice of creation. I am passion and peace, heart of dedication reading the intention of deeds.

I am the teardrops from their eyes, the struggle, and the strife. I am the finesse of weary sighs in this river called life.

I am joy. I am pain. I am lightning and thunder. I am the dance of the rain that rips hearts to shred. I am pompous. I am humble. I am the length of the warrior's step. I am the earthquake's lava.

I am satisfaction, and I am not regret.

I hear your cotton mouth, tongue to lips, vapid breath, deep inhales; the rapid word chatter that comes with your triggers.

I listen as you pontificate on narratives spun in your game. You never mention the innocent child or the victims with malleable minds.

All I see are the caverns and the darkness of your heart.

Keeper of Backwards Men

I held in my hand the daintiest of blossoms, fragile, needing constant attention and care to its small, velvety purple-hued head.

As I looked at it, I felt a mix of emotions. Frustration and adoration swept into one un-decipherable ball of colorful fractals. My want and yearning for its beauty kept it firmly in my palm, my lips blowing soft air against its petals.

I became lost in the soul of a flower.

Vennie Kocsis

I grab a handful of pillows and squeeze them until they break up into pieces resembling the shape of a human.

I am not sad. I am contemplative. I feel every strand of DNA in my body. I close my eyes, watching the molecules fall and rise, transforming the morning sun into an evening glow.

I am a droplet in a waterfall, a musical note contained within the lullaby of a siren.

Hold me tight. I am experiencing everything.

Keeper of Backwards Men

You are hiding behind a star, and I cannot find you through the maze of constellations. You are elusive. I climb the clouds, searching to find your eyes through the mist.

What is this place? I have found myself among the unknown, and I do not feel at home.

Come find me, lover. I am waning in the tide.

Piece by piece I melt into the cool swell. If only I could evaporate and return to the place of my birth where you wait to keep my soul safe from the harm of humans.

I enter the noiselessness. I see deeply. I know the truth. I am wise to transparency. I am not blind to its hiding. What odd pathways humans take when their whispers cause chaotic flux.

The hearer searches for the truth. Yet illusions are often interwoven inside of it, and the speaker plays games of pass-it-on as words become dangerously cryptic.

The mirror says beware. I nod in agreeable awareness. Situations are rarely as they seem and always exactly as I see. Behavioral observations are revealing.

Reactions become calculated, distant, and exact.

There are deceptions that circulate through history. Yet, remnants of evidence always find their way to shore as I explore the hallways of mirage memories.

I am content with being here. I do not partake in the disinterest and apathetic absence of spirit. I have seen into the ethereal strings of my universe.

I smile with knowing. I will continue to dance on this solitary raft. I have become skilled at loving myself. I need no lovers.

Vennie Kocsis

I am aware of strands, tree leaves that sway in the breeze, and every human face glancing in my direction.

Within these brief intervals I comprehend the language, manners of expression, and the circumstances of situations that are not mine.

My fingers start talking, leaking out feelings that stir the whirling universes beneath my rib cage. This is where it all starts.

I sit here by myself. I can confidently say that I am no longer lonely.

Keeper of Backwards Men

There is a musical song mixed with words, a guided symphony leaving me resolved inside of understanding.

A peace washes over me when her guidance becomes clear in raindrops on leaves and flower buds freshly opened.

I observe from a distance, feeling wistfulness brushing my neck. My mouth is alive with happiness as the path becomes clear like the sun.

Love blows freely, pushing matter aside. Parting heartaches like the Red Sea, she passes through me, a wayward butterfly refusing to die.

From the upper view there is a flash of soft lavender exuding into your skies. It is amassed across your planet.

If you choose to travel, please do, to a higher view, then look down upon your Earth. From this perspective the hue is completely different. It is a fireworks show of glowing souls.

No, your world is not ending. It is just the beginning.

Keeper of Backwards Men

Sink the fingers where the glass melts. Shimmering sunlight slides down my wrists. I am riding bliss like a time bomb.

Moments drift swift as the moonless night teases my angst. Strapped inside pyramids I die into the stars.

It all makes sense to those apparent. It all comes back three-fold, but it does not feel so certain when you're sitting alone.

At this stage in my life, I only want positive connections. I am done with pain, anger, divisiveness, and the maliciousness running amuck on the planet.

I want the mountains, flowers, trees, and the sea. I want relaxation and laughter. I want love that sees the good in others. I have no room left inside for the cold separation many humans have chosen to be absorbed in.

Healing is the only way to move consciousness forward.

Keeper of Backwards Men

You ask me who I am. I struggle for ways to put it into sentences short enough to not get tuned out. I shut down. I have been here through infinity, scribing, and creating databases of situations.

I overflow with the insensible ingesting. I am recycling energy into words, stored in images and cryptic, rhyming lines.

The ones stranded with me understand everything. Even if it is few, even if it is you, dive in. When you have reached the end, if you still have questions, I will answer in gematria.

Vennie Kocsis

Welcome to the upward slant. There is no going back.
Do not fight. Float. Do not grieve. You remain and
become the storm that blows away the battered form.

For you are seven colors of sky curved through
clouds. You are music and violins, soft chords, and
voices in harmony. You are the song of the universe.

Hi, sweet daughter. Remember me, back when it was, we managing the intricacies?

Remember flying away? It is all okay now. We can exhale into the flowers.

We miss you in the same way you do. You have been far away. Distant.

Tune in and listen. We have things to say, and you need to translate. Do not be afraid.

Vennie Kocsis

There are trees holding whispers of time, their leaves, remnants of words, dropped to the ground becoming dust and mulch.

There are people letting out anguish against the rough bark, tears letting out the pains in their tender hearts.

There are backs relaxed into the curves reading books on summer days, letting the world drift away.

Who cannot love the tree, never abandoning, always there, waiting without judgment as we spill out our deepest parts.

Keeper of Backwards Men

There are layers of skin where sight lives. You look with your eyes. I see with my senses. I observe in silence as the violence unearths itself brick by brick.

You are ocean and love's hoping. You are crystalline and laughter. There is a glow in you that is increasing as the scattered thoughts cease their screaming.

You are the calm of midnight. You are the warrior's valiant fight. When you have reached the center of you, that's when it all subdues.

Keeper of Backwards Men

I am not taken in by tokens or false hoping. I drift along with the presence of the now. Each moment is independent of the other. I am my own father and mother. I was designed, and in this reality, there is no blame, only acceptance.

I am not ashamed of the rivers and rocks that damaged my skin. I rejuvenate my being from within.

Vennie Kocsis

Kneel with your elders, the empaths of time. Learn the linear truths which have been kept from you.

Inhale and let the oxygen increase each individual cell. Create a wider swell to let the knowledge expel.

You are brilliant, divine, and complicated, a rabbit hole not just anyone can explore. Stay individual inside the one, love.

Keeper of Backwards Men

Aloneness is pertinent. There was a day I went nowhere for a very long time.

Where is nowhere? On the edge of sanity, where all the color and magic reside?

It is the aftermath of infinity, being no one, and nothing for too long.

Vennie Kocsis

Red is the blood dancing through me and orange is my sunset.

Blue is my melancholy and violet my severance of free.

My color has its own definition. My rainbows do not arch. They have edges, sharp and wordless, dripping water for thirsting.

We are all, in the end, collecting masses of data taking different forms.

As space, molecules, atoms, anti-matter, and all that is, we exist as unending shape shifters.

Humans measure with time, then waste it.

I smile. I open the pieces, doing the work to stay alive inside.

Word by word. Thought by thought. Talk by talk.

Conversations bring acceptance where there is no judgment.

I will never be who I once was, fermented and worried, manic, and chaotic. I flow inside this lavender glow.

Day by day.

    Minute by minute.

        Winning by winning.

Keeper of Backwards Men

I may choose to drown here in ocean waves all legs, arms, and sea swept hair. I may suddenly choose to evaporate; become breeze, breathing, and seeing.

With just the spark of telepathy, I become whatever I draw in. It's all the essence.

Vennie Kocsis

Endlessness is filled with rhythm and prisms.

I am home no matter where I roam because life is always surging. I was born with portals for DNA, and so I travel the waves through distance and time.

Keeper of Backwards Men

I am a solid mass of muted aftermath. I will not bend. I will not bow.

I will not pray to cowards who fabricate in attempts to intimidate. I will not bend.

I am not what is thought. I have always fought. I will not bend. I will not run.

Arrows shot to wound me bounce off and only bruise me. I do not bend. I do not break. Even when my heart aches.

Radiance gathers like water and seashore, building more.

Moving sand and stone we build homes from ashes and disaster.

We are warrior and depth, adept at flying, hiding, smiling, and telepathically speaking. We are new to you. What to do? What to do?

What you know as one has become many, and such is the life of being in multiple realities.

4. WOMANHOOD

wom·an·hood
/ˈwoomən͵(h)ood/
noun
the state or condition of being a woman.

Newness is not a gateway into perfection. I was created in a nontypical birth.

"It's an ease," he said, "a walk, a step, a way about your temperament."

Keeper of Backwards Men

We talked about otherkin, lifeforms, star seeds and such. You remembered the past lives like it was tomorrow. I feel silent inside words. I am always hushed there.

We parted ways simply. I remained in the moment bringing no urgency or awareness of time.

It was what it was.

There is a stillness that has come over me here, drawing energy likewise.

Like minds. Like smiles. Like raindrops soft on my face.

Vennie Kocsis

When women age, we become crones, silver witches who have learned to love the lines on our eyes, grooves in our skin, quieter temperaments. We lose track of time.

When women age, we learn that laughing with a sisterhood can make up for lonely empty beds, and conversations held over shot glasses, meals cooked with secrets, leave us unaware of trivial things; like what other people think about our existence.

When women age, we become invisible ghosts walking over hills. We are mirages, porcelain masks with chipped edges. We learn to submerge into the deepness of sleep somewhere in the ocean where youthfulness does not exist and skeletons live for centuries.

Keeper of Backwards Men

The problem was not the money or the fame, not the
taunt ripe bruises shining from her heart or the
painful creak of her hip bones when she moved.

It was not the seeping words or the tightness in her
chest every time she passed a church, not the way the
holiday lights made her head dizzy or the faraway
sensations in grocery store lines.

It was not the smell of soap or staring for hours
at the ceiling; not the smooth metal of the numbing
pipe or sweet tastes of sangria wine.

Not the many ways she had been used or the
indignation that set in when the walls were empty, not
the comparisons or the dismissive tendencies, the
disconnections draining her energy or even the
isolation.

It was not meditation or constant spirit speak,
not the unpaid bills on the mahogany desk or the
whirring sounds of a radiator about to explode
in her only transportation. It was not the way she
robotically moved through her day or the smiles she
feigned, not the glow in her eyes left by too many
nights of crying or the sleep making memories fade.

The problem was the sadness living there in the base
of her spine like a tall thin castle spearing up into her
vertebrae until her whole being ached.

He told me that he was hoping bread would come my way. He wished even harder that the birds did not eat it.

If he only knew, it is not the birds that ruin the bread.

The rain does.

I realized how different our lives are and how unforgiving flipped around love is, a liar with a happy go lucky face smiling for everyone to see, taunting, stealing hearts, and creating misery.

How dare he?

This eve you will be sitting with your circle cutting your eyes to the lady at the corner bar, wondering if she is noticing you like you see her. You will leave late because you did not have the guts.

Afternoon is supposed to bring delight. I ramble on cuz the page is all I have. I cannot eat because my tummy is churning. Sometimes I miss inner coldness.

Tonight, I am glad I am not freezing.

Keeper of Backwards Men

I wish I could tell her what I see, the capabilities, how I watch her bent knees dejected, and it kills me.

I observe across miles. She never sees me hovering, assessing, and seeing the future when she is through it.

She is every woman in pain, processing the angst, which settles in when life changes. We rearrange ourselves to rise out of hell.

She is the moon, distant, fighting resistance to become the sun, and I believe in her strength to find herself again.

I wish I could tell her, "you got this" without sounding dismissive. So, I gaze through stars, and I cheer her on.

Self-blame settles into the skin. It becomes ley lines of DNA cells mapping time and possibilities.

More than sight can see or ears can hear she holds the scent of Spring in her palms.

"Run, little girl, run. Go to the hills and into the trees where no one can find you, and you will be free."

Keeper of Backwards Men

She has never longed for the absence of voices as much as she does right now. She has never longed for the dominance of debate, the strained conversation, the hesitancy of departure and a severance of connection, as much as she does right now.

She feels sad, empty, distant, lost, and abandoned.

She moves between moments of wanting to turn away forever and this uncontrollable force that pulls like a magnet, chains that lock her into this place. She wants to beg for attention, yet longs to not be scrutinized. She wants to smell, to taste, to feel, to accept, long and to belong.

She smiles beyond every weight the world could place on her back, glowing in happiness, while aching inside. She has never felt so average and absent from beauty. To herself, she is nameless, faceless, just an ordinary failure in a world of success, even as her accomplishments lay before her.

Everything inside of her, consumed. Her hands cling to ropes gripped tightly in her palms, holding to the possibility of someday, cursing the weakness prohibiting her permanent exit. A slave to her imagination, soul is the only sparkle in her eye, and driven by love, she survives.

There is a sea of aloneness bearing its waves against her back. She is there in each ticking second of ordinary and unordinary days.

There are whispers coming through.

Do they speak the truth? Can she trust you?

Keeper of Backwards Men

I am abandoned. She has left me. It has been seven years. I have cried enough tears to fill a new ocean. I still cling to waves, a slowly deflating raft.

    I am to blame.

She has left me with the aftermath, another useless item. I should have been softer, but instead I was more outspoken.

I was a tyrant who lacked good judgment. Self-hatred develops into a river that flows in the opposite direction, preventing it from ever reaching the sea.

Now, it is just these walls and me, acting like we are a whole being when really, I am fragments strewn about in a disorganized manner.

I can feel you pulling away from me. You are going back to them, back to the suffocating caverns that are so familiar. You have decided that the fear of the unknown is greater than the pain that you have endured.

I reclaim the coldness so that I do not have to continue holding this.

Next round the pain will be worse. It will beat you until your knees shake, even though you said you were done with heartache. I wonder how much more you will be able to take and if you will outlive the emotional rape.

I have a journey I must create, so I cannot stay, sweet sister. I cannot keep holding space.

I yearn as the tides turn to become the ash; we burned in the anticipation that your loneliness would not become excuses. I continue with my mission, but first I must try to cry.

I am half a century old. Where exactly am I going from here? I foresee myself sipping something while sitting on a back porch lit with citronella candles.

I always imagined that when I got older, I would crave a more free-spirited lifestyle. Now, all I want is peace and laughter, moments to myself, and opportunities to create art, music, and writing.

I am reliving my childhood. I have created for myself the setting of a fantastic land. I am a fighter, a dancer, and a song lover, keeping my arms open to promise.

Vennie Kocsis

She hangs from the eave, hovering, wanting to be seen by me, and I wince inwardly.

I remind myself that she is the reason I have moments of freezing dead in my skin and how hard I have fought to win.

Without emotion, I leave her restless in eternal commotion.

Keeper of Backwards Men

To the girl who told me secrets I said I would keep.

To the girl who made me laugh despite her pain and the aftermath.

To the girl who keeps her dreams in the thunder of her screams.

To the girl who watches in the distance tethered to compliance.

I can speak so you will never be left silent.

Vennie Kocsis

What wistful ways lovers dance, eyes intense, falling into a trance, bent like trees, branches extending their never-ending adoration.

What an invisible life. She never thought she would wince at humans holding hands with bonded elegance.

She searched the earth in caves, slept through pitch black nights, her hands empty, holding dust and aloneness.

The human aches. She wishes to soothe her, to become form, hold her close so she can feel chosen just once. But she is destined for strangers wandering in and out as though her heart is a brick door.

Young, she will escape, finish this cycle soon, return home where her legs do not ache from running, and her ear will not ring from screaming. There, her breath becomes a blanket wrapped tight so she can sleep.

Now we pass between these worlds. We see through, beyond, between, beneath and inside, smiling through the tears we hide.

Keeper of Backwards Men

You are a different kind of damaged, chaotic mind.

I see the reflection as your soul dies

   lie,
    by lie,
     by lie.

There is pain too deep to touch, an abyss in your untethered loneliness.

I feel slightly stoic and disinterested, an odd reaction, to not feel sorry for the churning of your own hurting.

When irradiation glimmers inside the air you call darkness, is it safer there?

I am swiftly running out of time, must focus forward, head held high as I silently take the podium to speak.

Empowered woman. Empowered me.

Vennie Kocsis

I am a woman born from the womb of struggle, demand, and circumstance. I have fought the raging oceans to find a home.

I am a woman glittering love amongst the sadness. I am a proud warrior of all that is right, daughter of the Moon, sister of the Light.

I am a woman bearing scars upon her skin, marks that speak of childbirth, tattooed tales of a journey filled with experience.

I am a woman whose body holds no criticism, mother of madness and sovereign witch.

I call it individuality.

You call it difference.

Get up, girl. My breath becomes plastic, plastered disaster, lain across a mattress, twisted in sheets.

Get up, girl. My heart beats faster, rapid brain waves leaking thoughts strained from overloaded pain.

Get up, girl. Whispers climb the walls in a fogged-out haze. Some days blend in warped place.

Get up, girl. Walk the paths. Bring yourself back from the past and years of depression. This session is over.

Get up, girl. Walk the beach. Touch the trees. Remember your sovereignty is your magic and self-care, a habit.

Get up, girl.

Vennie Kocsis

The girl in the black dress is face down in the dirt, smothering while the oblivious dances.

Red lipstick doesn't just leave stains on collars.

The girl in the black dress, they said was just different, walked around silent, notebooks under arms, and pens in her hair like porcupine quills.

The girl in the black dress had one for every weekday. Sunday was the lace collar to keep her close enough to Father.

The girl in the black dress liked pink more than anything,

"Pep-to dismal," Mama said.

"Black is more slimming. Especially for a girl like you."

A girl like you, incapable, unlovable girl.

The girl in the black dress lives drenched in loneliness, just her, shelves of journals documenting the pain, a closet of dresses and fading lipstick, becoming invisible, like their interest.

Keeper of Backwards Men

Pardon me, sir. Can i get a break from this heart ache? Fuck this solitary trail, these shitty memories of forests when I was trapped breaking bread with bears.

You weren't there. Don't nod your head like you understand. I was an ancient woman before you ever became a man.

You might be a tsunami or you could be a raft to safety. There are phrases, trigger situations that make her step back. She finds balance with the sea and forest, rarely with other humans.

Often taken personally, she becomes wary. She knows what she carries; what she protects. One wrong step, and she is quietly observing again.

She doesn't follow leaders. She is her own guru. You will create a perception of her, and it will become your truth.

She has almost reached exceptional solitude. She is distant and feeling in reverse. She swiftly re-stabilizes her skies.

Keeper of Backwards Men

There are grave consequences for actions, and sometimes they get passed on to the next generation.

Mistakes can't be erased. Absolution is a figment of your imagination, so I say proceed with caution.

She will spend the remaining years in communication with the wheel members, existing together in conversations unheard and misunderstood by humans. They will create an impenetrable wall too high for the eyes of predatory passersby.

She will dive inside the pupils of women who silently weep.

She will long for home daily, actively keeping up with the present, founded by the past, carving new paths in the stone walls she frequently encounters.

Lights in the clouds will become consistent reminders, and the trees will become her reprieve.

This, her chosen destiny.

This distant, unknown feeling, I am daughter to a host. I cannot connect my soul, never recall the soft loving arms of her. She is fog wisps blowing distant, narcissistic, and wounded.

Vennie Kocsis

I am a woman with a thousand lifetimes of history flowing through me like watered down mercury.

If you don't choose to see me, I can't carry the blame, and if you choose to abuse me, I won't carry the shame.

I see her there weeping. She is repeating all the mistakes that make her ache, but it's not up to me to provide relief.

Vennie Kocsis

I am rebelling. I am redirecting. I am watching the doers. Nothing is more important than focusing on my creativity. Who will be waiting when I emerge from hibernation?

Not everything is meant to be. It is up to me to choose the best route and weed out what is not contributing to my mission.

Somewhere in the corner of a cafe, a table waits for a girl with fingers ready to pound keys and tell the rest of her story.

Keeper of Backwards Men

What does it feel like to be a ghost shunned, a soul ungrieved, not missed and unforgiven?

In the hovering bowels of mysticism where the cynics hang their hats, she waits to be acknowledged.

There is satisfaction in a conscious reaction, when the spirit feels wishing just like we did when we were young and missing.

Vennie Kocsis

There is a summer awaiting fingers debating word phrases as I disengage from the grid and go in.

In the meantime, I hold you at distances. Not because I don't love you. I don't trust you.

Loyalty is not given. It is earned. The world can burn tomorrow, and the hollow earth can explode. Wars can be waged and chemicals sprayed.

Who will be there to hold you?

Her human heart smarts at moments captured by lovers, gazes of adoration she has never received, and she will split her existence away from the dimension where she doesn't feel welcomed.

I am a board, flat, emotionless. I am searching clouds to find smiles. Humans are often disappointing creatures. What a demented feature to embed into DNA.

Why? So, we can ache?

There aren't many years left. Forty years will leave in a blink. She will adventure alone, finding no companion to dive in the seas. She leaves them in the shallows to go dance in the coral reefs.

Vennie Kocsis

Braving human existence with the horror and the persistence of struggle, she will crawl through mud, huddled in corners, and stand on mountain tops screaming for the humans to stop.

Days will become a continuum of traveling into the blackness where dreams reveal truth.

Absent for days; tear letting, she will not spend any more moments on regretting.

Vennie Kocsis

5. INHERENT

in·her·ent
/inˈhirənt,inˈherənt/
adjective
existing in something as a permanent,
essential, or characteristic attribute.

I stand on cliffs, hands on hips, face lifted towards twilight. Let the moonlight in. Time to cleanse again. No more sin.

I write endings to new beginnings.

Interesting. It doesn't really hurt.

Life just feels different.

Sometimes the voice of the world drowns out the voice of the inner god. The whispers of shame can rule a life, taunting with fear of judgment and the secrets we hold.

It is through expressionism that I have survived.

I've put to rest my shame, letting it go to find its own home. Now, I write my pages out to comfort newly seeping hearts.

Vennie Kocsis

Who can take into their hands such a fragile existence as ours? Who can be worthy of this synergy? Spun, we ring the bells of vibrational cyclone spells.

Not all that exists is intended. Some are pretended, and this circle of light, pure amethyst, serves and protects us.

What immortal ways lovers recycle each other. Like magnets they cannot avoid the passings, broken rafts adrift a sea, leaving mystery to be discovered by another.

Keeper of Backwards Men

So much they don't know. How I do numeric license plate reduction to get through traffic, count my breaths in grocery store lines to stay in control of an agoraphobic mind. How my ear buzzes when the sound is too loud, and I cannot hear my own volume. So, my voice elevates and irritates the unknowing.

I pack my bags for the faithful woods where trees accept me for me, and flowers smile, even on rainy days, because in these breakable moments, I have paid atonement for graven mistakes made from a mind riddled with bullet holes.

When they want you to fold in like a tiny infant, and they want your voice to be low, if not silent, just go.

Healing is a decision, one made with such precision, the path cannot be altered. When the truth sinks in and the fodder isn't enough for an empty belly, sorrow searches for a home.

Sometimes that means choosing a life of being alone.

Your clock hands will soon stop moving as time becomes non-existent. Imagine a reality where you flow inside of **only** what makes you joyful.

Are you still struggling to understand this state of being?

Here acceptance is needed.

Keeper of Backwards Men

The day I disappeared and became invisible was the moment I became invincible.

I got lost inside the existence of my absence. I disappeared, and it brought me here.

Now I stand unexpected, affected and feeling.

I am healing.

It is said the sum of the numb means we have succumbed to acceptance. I call that self-rejecting.

I will fade into the distance. I am no longer resisting the calls to explore caves lined with files of memories.

The day I disappeared; the world was quiet. My face never reached a scream. I became an echo of a dream, a memory slowly merging into remnants of words melting into the earth.

Vennie Kocsis

My heart break makes me choke, an aching they will never know. So much whining about the trials of their life. You give me your childhood, and I'll give mine. We'll take measure of who really survived.

Shattered wood returns to earth quickly. It becomes dust and ash, disappearing. One day they will sit around musing how I used to be the tallest tree.

Keeper of Backwards Men

The tears don't come so easily. I push them away,
barely breathing, as the nights steal their possibility.

I am left in a desert of reality.

I have no regret with being open. I hold no angst,
laying my neck against a guillotine to have the chance
to touch a soul.

I listen to absorb a little more, let it melt its way down
into my core where raindrops laugh and avoid spilling
into the sea.

Stop trying to fix the broken hearted with your big words.

Until you've worn the shoes of a human's abuse, speech is mere syllables and letters leaving the lips of ones who can never really know.

Stop trying to proselytize those who have survived. We're not meant to be guinea pigs for psychologists.

Keeper of Backwards Men

Don't speak of me in terms of irrelevance. You don't know how I flow waterfalls of knowledge, perspective, and intelligence.

Excuse my elegance. You mistook me for weak. Beware of how you speak. You stand too firmly in quicksand disguised as alibis.

The truth will stand a chance when your ego finds balance.

I stand here in a universe defined as human. My identity rises as I scribe the pain of the past and the collective aching of these masses.

I become static. There is no competition in healing. There is only steadiness and acceptance.

Each earth being is uniquely complete as we find our way back to our own sacred, geometric biology.

Keeper of Backwards Men

I fall asleep at moonrise and awaken at thrice night where everything goes quiet. I can walk away any day. I can turn my face toward the places I seek out information, and truth about this existence.

I'm about to tell the stories. I used to sing the blues to avoid it. But my gears are ticking, and I'm getting fickle.

I reach up into midnight skies, touch the moonlight and cry. I want to return home.

I go back to those moments and sit inside the hopelessness. It is good to remember this; to never forget lest I leave behind the reasons why I fight.

Don't get stuck in chaos. Release comes easily. Find the reason. Each day repeats. I train. I don't accept defeat.

Into the wind I send the dissonance. Take your fear and continual offense at every statement to the quagmire where it belongs.

Silence. Repose. Retreat.

Dead or alive the hive will continue to speak the truth about you.

Keeper of Backwards Men

There is something about nothingness. It teaches lessons. It reminds me to be humble. I am no one in a world of humans trying to be everyone.

So many trails hold the wails and raindrops that fell from eyes hanging in bodies trying to stay alive.

So much headache.

So much unnecessary horror. I wonder. What happened to the heart of mankind to make it turn vile? What switch got flipped and created these villains?

Keeper of Backwards Men

Chess boards have become violin cords. I pluck the strings, singing myself into where acceptance has good posture, healing is my father, letting go is my mother, and holding you accountable is my brother.

I am adding spines to this memoir of lessons as the air flows through my chest.

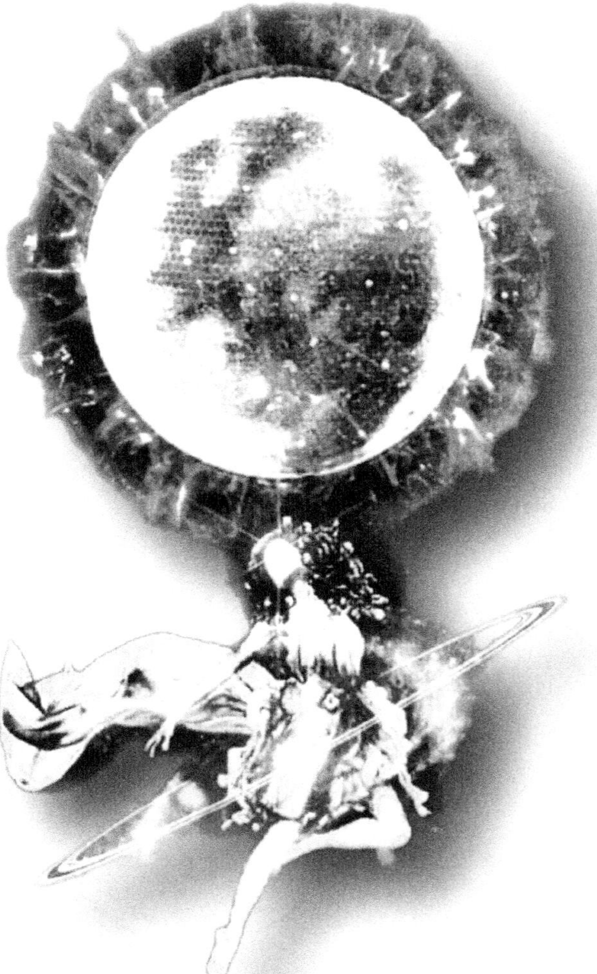

6. NUMINOUS

nu·mi·nous
/ˈnoomənəs/
adjective
having a strong religious or spiritual quality.
indicating or suggesting the presence of a divinity.

Vennie Kocsis

A glimpse out of the corner of my eye revealed the sunniest of sunflowers, swaying in the breeze next to me and beaming through its star-kissed face.

I delightedly turned around to return the smile. Hands made of leaves reached up into its center and removed a seed from. The leafy hand gently held my hair as it inserted the seed into my mouth before moving on. I wanted to concentrate on the delicious flavor, so I closed my eyes.

At that precise moment, I had to decide between the pain I was holding and the imposing structure of life in front of me, inviting me to approach.

I took the tiny seedling out of my mouth and placed it in my pocket before taking a step towards the opportunities being presented.

Keeper of Backwards Men

Everyone wants the truth until it is pointed at you, until the face must reverse to moments of receiving and causing hurt.

Go inside. Figure out why the seeking; the aching; the wanting; the taking, the breaking, the lashing out, the separating, the lack of loyalty, the dedication, the restoration, the reverberations, and illumination.

We don't know all. Listen to the inner call. Your spirit is speaking.

Reclaim, and be strong. Stand still in the silent amniotic fluid, plasma, and colors of arrays that warm the face. As you debate, a mirror awaits. Shed your skin and go within.

Vennie Kocsis

There are ghosts in my view. I am traveling in the hallways. We are coming back for you. Your breath quickens as you wait. Will your heart give in to the ache from the secrets you hold?

They rot your insides, you know. We are your shadow self.

Every deed, word, blow, and theft of innocence lurks inside the remnants of your biological cells. You never considered that hell would come from those you desecrated.

We have gathered the ashes of our pasts, reconstructed our wings, and are prepared to fly.

We are the offspring of your terror, the outcasts and sinners, scar bearers and wayward waifs. We are the tattooed tyrants, born from your horror, walking our own paths against your wrath. We know each step with precision as we enter this fight.

We are not mercy. We are strength.

We are not bitter. We are valiant.

We release shame. It is not ours. It belongs to you. Your turn to be burdened with your own deeds is long overdue.

Inspect the words returned, the lines unspoken, and the invisible fences rushing electricity through your stomach without warning.

I am a lurker in the shadows, a mystic of the hovering corners. The view is clear up here. I see the past and futures merging. I feel the sadness and pain purging.

I hear every heart hurting from the wicked to the wounded and my eyes focus on the cries of the affected, injected by decades of apathetic sociopathy using human flesh in the deadliest fashions.

You will relax, forget to watch your back, and we will attack, because you deserve to be fought. You deserve to be blessed with unrest.

Welcome to the Resurrection.

Keeper of Backwards Men

Don't give way to fear, dears. See the beauty around you. In mindful observation you will increase your own illumination. When you see yourself the same as we see you, you will no longer be confused.

Vennie Kocsis

We are pensive, hidden, purposely unnoticed, only speak of it to each other.

We write it, paint it, and sing it.

They are unfocused, organized religious zealots, diabolical replicas, rendered children of Zion, angered by the uncontrolled.

We will gather, make no mistake, you with your held out crosses, and your black thumping books spewing scriptures that choke out truth.

We are the Mystics, the witch's brew, the keeper of their thoughts, and holders of the knowing. We are the Old World tenderly tossed with the New, a salad of scrolls garnished with wisdom and dressed in apparitions that they call ghosts.

There is a fire sparking in the mountains. I see them dancing, eyes wild with love and energy, hands raised, hips moving in rhythm with their own beat. I smile at the divinity as they find absolution in the composition of their feet.

Keeper of Backwards Men

I turn the knobs, tune the strings so I can sing my way through all the things I never tell you. Like how I need to be alone with a solitary soul singing lullabies to the infinite sky.

Vennie Kocsis

There are witches who remember the stars long before humans tried to eliminate them and morph them into storm clouds.

We are the love healers and defenders of the innocent, hurt and harmed. We are highly skilled in defense, both physically and infinitely. We can never be killed.

Inside of perceived weakness is great strength. We will lift the clutter from the gutters that have been ruthlessly torn into this Earth. We are her rebirth, the rising of a righteous generation no book has ever written.

Everything you see is exceptionally new, even the reflection looking back at you.

Keeper of Backwards Men

I take this life seriously.

I have no tolerance for war games, I am fighting real battles. No tolerance for the unsupportive who flee when the cages rattle.

If I go ghost into the fog and become a mirage, I'll never return to disappointing the idealistic who created an image of me; so unrealistic.

I'm a million scattered pieces. My body struggles weakly. Swimming through the mud, gathering remnants, I am picking each one up.

I will sew them back together into a magical collection.

Vennie Kocsis

Rock the sadness, my love. Hold it bravely in your tender arms. It is an infant you can re-love.

Fly with the visions, sweet thrivers. Take back your mind. Release the ghosts. You are no longer the forgotten lamb in the chains of monsters and madness.

Command the past and swaddle the deepest parts of your gentle heart.

Keeper of Backwards Men

There is a world around us. It breathes and weeps. It is filled with open wounds and pain that seeps.

I hold moments in my palms like diamonds that teach me to smile so the rough waters will calm.

I wash tears with compassion, and sprinkle relief on lowered faces. I am passing out rations, a taste of a new day.

I am awakened to my worth as actions blend with words and beauty comes in forms of laughter as we love freely.

Earth has gifted us infinite possibilities.

Walk with me beside the ocean. It's been a while since we've spoken. I was hoping we could remember the days when we danced together.

Vennie Kocsis

In the distance, the future glistens, a prism, a beauty inside my breathlessness. This is never all there is.

Behind the glass I stand, protected and observatory in an unfolding story of a life survived by lessons.

Keeper of Backwards Men

Do not follow another's soul. You may end up inside of an abyss for which there is no return. Instead, sit with your own mind. Release influence and go inside of your questions. Everything has a solution.

Don't worship another human for their promises. You are wasting worry focused on unknown futures; days better spent exploring your present.

Still the skin. Listen without opinion.

Standing inside of smoke for too long will deaden your lungs. Staring in mirrors will desensitize your humility.

You know what you need to do to be free.

Release Belief.

Vennie Kocsis

Who stole your pearls?

Who ripped into your shell without mercy, leaving you shattered, thirsting, and mourning?

Who broke you and told you that you weren't the ALL-SUPREME of your own being?

Who closed your eyes; made your love die, until every cell, each fiber, ached from the heartbreak?

Who reminds you of your exquisite existence?

Who holds the mirror to your spirit?

How often do you go silent, waiting to hear it?

Who taught you validation comes from confirmations outside of your own musical lips?

You are a gift. Sing to your ability, for you are fulfilling the path which you have chosen to morph into being. You are freeing your love, one stumble at a time.

Stay steady on the climb. You have almost arrived.

I am a seer. I carry no crystal ball. I feel it all, the whispering vibrations of energy passing, a consistent inspiration for craving quiet.

I am an integrated introvert immersed in the colors keeping my sanity intact.

Piece together the fettered fragments you were shattered into. Glue them with gold. Build yourself into a work of art like no other, unique and unto yourself.

You have been given the colors of sunrises and sunsets. My friends, come forth into your worth. You are Kings and Queens of your own BE-ing.

An embodied empath doesn't waver. They fight clairvoyantly, using their minds.

They speak truth and stand inside authenticity with no shame or fear, building boundaries allowing nothing or anyone to make them open their gates.

They know limits and when to wait. They are not afraid to walk away.

The embodied empath accepts themself and makes their own trail. They see deep and don't care who doesn't believe.

They know intuition is magic and choose wisely for the betterment of their own growth.

Please don't waste another minute not feeling it all. Open the doors of your spirit. Let the filled rooms empty and the empty rooms become filled. Engage in the thrill of a human experience.

Be endearing to you. Laugh with your stumbles. Hug your worry. Dance with your teardrops. Snuggle with your fear. Skip with your joy, and in all, make each minute matter.

Welcome to the healing wheel where we learn to deal with sorrow and expect tomorrow to be better, unfettered and released from the chains that were created from the pain of dis-ease.

Energy is food and magnetic matter. That which is powered increases. Either you are dining on love or you are food for fear.

Which are you choosing?

Your decisions are challenged by the choice of rejecting everything clouding your inner self.

Keeper of Backwards Men

You love through clouds and space, across electronic grids and wind. You meet in dream realms, making love in the color. You are formed, yet formless. You who understand this, connect in the most beautiful ways.

Vennie Kocsis

She can no longer couple with human genetics; cannot allow the entrance or the convolution of her elegance. She holds shields because the charming deserts are killing fields.

She looks back on the ways she tried to be human; begged for acceptance from people shooting bullets riddled with rejection, and she understands the path more clearly.

She is a fully bloomed Empath, fourth dimensional perspective where the rejection doesn't make her wince as it once did.

She roams wooded trails alone. The trees and clouds, her home. She gazes at the moon, Artemis smiling through the night sky.

It is almost time.

She goes astral, flying through skies, past the stars and through the gate where her otherkin waits.

Keeper of Backwards Men

Sometimes the ugliest parts of us can be the most beautiful when refined. Our anger, polished and contained, becomes unquenchable passion. That fear we try and hide becomes signals of reality verses confusion. The scars become a roadmap of survival and triumph.

We display ourselves, raw and skinless for all to see. It's the best we can be, freely moving inside our vulnerability.

Live each breath the best. Love your shine with the same fervor you choose to hate your darkness. Soon your heart will be so bright, your skin will shimmer with the newness of your brilliant life.

Vennie Kocsis

Reckoning has many faces, unexpected veils and illusions that become intrusions leaving the unprepared affected.

The egoist is off kilter inside the self-righteous fodder of an imaginary, sadistic Father. Fear the fray that is sewn back together, for it can bear the weight of many lives. It turns swiftly, gaining strength and paving ways.

Breaking bones in the falls, we shatter lies like rolling logs. We are on the walk, in our own body, always on the move, distantly watching you.

Keeper of Backwards Men

Let your tears flow joy and your mouth speak truth.
Let your eyes see all and your ears hear you.

Then you will fall in love with feeling your inner healing, staying within the glow of all that you know.

Vennie Kocsis

I go silent sometimes.

I ask myself, "am I paralyzed inside?"

I feel speechless, no words, just forced rhymes.

I go hide sometimes, needing complete quiet to contemplate life. So many possibilities. Which way will I fly?

I became old before I was born, emerged into gravity, a fire filled storm. I am water and calm seas. An invincible, contemplative visionary.

7. GUARDIAN

guard·i·an
/ˈgärdēən/
noun
a defender, protector, or keeper.

Vennie Kocsis

They ask me why I am so distant. I sit in the misinterpretation of my fears and caution. Converse with me of the weather, of the beauty of the mountains, the shimmering way the sun beats off the closing in of the gray clouds and the sounds of the city.

They tell me of their youth. I give them allowable, pre-approved selections of my own to hold.

Do not invite me to tea. I will not go beyond streetlights and graveled driveways.

I shiver against my own coldness. I want what I should not want, a constant war of wills inside my mind.

These lies destroy me, pulling me in navigation towards something I have no realization of. The warmth of my open window beats onto my naked arms, candle breath blowing sweet scents into my nostrils, and every single sliding thought encompasses a face that I need to run towards.

Speak to me and tell me that this will be okay; that this just needs patience.

Keeper of Backwards Men

If you wanna be on this earth, kid, you gotta grow some backbone and acceptance. The most you'll ever be to me are lines in a poem, verses in a song, sentences in a story, and fuel for creativity.

You are oil. I am water. You're dead weight. I am the daughter of life, a chosen one.

You are larvae.

I am reborn.

Vennie Kocsis

I organize information into various dossiers, recordings of the files just in case it's necessary to jog someone's memory.

Is that something that you find bothersome, surface swimmer?

You shouldn't try to con a seer. Be cautious about the battles you pick. I am adept at addressing behaviors that are sparked from feelings of self-shame.

Warrior here I stand not regretting any love that has been given. If conflict is what you seek, I am willing to disengage.

I have nothing to hide. I am crafty at my game. I've put intention into my training.

If this is what malevolence wants, then so mote it will be.

Attack me. I will walk away laughing.

Keeper of Backwards Men

Stay shine zoned, child. Stay wild and true. We will meet in the flowers real soon. It will be a delight to be in respite.

You're doing great.

Stay focused on the mission. Don't forget your intermissions of rest and self-recognition.

Walls lined with pull out scrolls, the gentle pages unfold. They hold thousands of years, stories never told to human ears.

Societies keep the secrets of the ones who live below where the tunnels are still, and the rooms vast and hollow. There are whispers in the streets, but none dare knock to enter the inner-earth monastery.

Keeper of Backwards Men

I sit in the silence of a million swirling thoughts, not accepting this separation, and chewing on the assumptions like they are the last supper.

I kneel beside a flower. She is starting to die. I hold her lovingly as her petals cry. I wish to breathe for every piece that has expired, wish to love for every soul weary and tired.

I open my arms to receive the Moon. I am spiraling sunlight where my skin is anew.

I let me become me, one with the trees as they renewed my soul's divinity.

Vennie Kocsis

When your tribe is true there is no dramaturgy playing violin strings or symphonies. All are at peace with each being who we are.

Witch. Warlock. Children of the Stars. Daughters of the Moon. Sisters to the Trees. Shapeshifters. Love Givers. Moniceptors. Otherkin. Indigos. Crystals.

We are at differing levels of growth actualization. We have varying age ranges. We are a wise and skilled tribe. We rise.

Keeper of Backwards Men

I wish to be unaffected and ejected into the spaces where nothing phases me. I send the memories away, an abandoned, jaded daughter who was led to the slaughter violently.

He held me beneath the waters until the bubbles ceased to float. I had given up hope.

But you, misted memories, you left me here unclean in the place where the scars have seams. People walk into each other's lives, stretch their hearts open, embedding knives disguised as compliments.

I touch the flesh-like roses and breathe the scent because in the end all that's left are the causes and effects.

Vennie Kocsis

Alone, I wait for the seasons while all around me mouths drip with treason, knives sticking into backs as they lay dying in their own malice.

I don't know if there's redemption for choices gone stone, or if seeds can push their way out of crevices that don't exist, because from where I sit it's a balancing trick between passion, weeping and heartlessness.

Keeper of Backwards Men

To be a warrior, one must learn to wait silently in the shadows. We gather our energy into the arching pull back of our bows. We watch. We observe. We do not fall into senses of time.

To be a warrior one paints themselves into the colors of their own vulnerability, disallowing shame, or the blaming of victims. We gather information, build dossiers, leaving factually scribed scrolls of truth in secret rooms.

The warrior is not quick to react, but instead, a steady pace of actions well thought out and enacted.

To be a warrior, one must survive and stay alive inside the turmoil of human bile. We see the thing for what it is and do not let our minds rest inside of unrealistic expectations. We gain evidence from behaviors.

To be a warrior, sometimes we have to say goodbye.

Vennie Kocsis

Somewhere there's sleep waiting for me, there's dreaming and dying, and gold carpet riding, For now I follow. I'm ripe for the chore when you meet me at midnight to settle this score.

Keeper of Backwards Men

Humans have a need to believe in anything, something, outside of the truth of who they are. It's a sad state of a nation, the planetary devastation, and she feels each heart caving.

I remind her of home where there are no religions or rituals, no groups separating one from another or elevated egos. She keeps her eyes on the color, waiting to swim in the plasma, each stroke a whisper against her skin. She breathes deeply, exhaling her humanness.

It is the life of an otherkin, earthly hybrid, walking among the human ones, unnoticed and undetected, save the green reflected in her emotional eyes.

Anger is a self-destructive projection with no ethics or critical thinking. It impulsively acts without consideration of consequence.

Learn the power of calm and winning a mental war. It's the art of strategy. It is an expensive thought process. It is a lack of being quick to react.

The people in my circle must be warriors who contain and maintain the passion to fight and go to battle. My army is small, yet impenetrable. Everyone else is a molecular extension.

Loyalty is pertinent during these times, protecting the spirit and the mind.

Vennie Kocsis

I disengage from the grid and go in. I hold you at distances because I don't trust you.

The world can burn tomorrow, and the hollow earth can explode. Wars could be waged and chemicals sprayed. Observe the words returned, the lines unspoken, the invisible fences that rush electricity through your stomach without warning.

In these times you gotta be on your own side.

Keeper of Backwards Men

You are searching. You have read as much as you can, sifting through the many words, discerning fact from fiction. Some things feel familiar. Other information leaves a questionable doubt.

If there is ever a moment to listen to your intuition it is now. Every single answer you seek is already coded into the parts of your DNA you have been told you cannot access.

Small platoons take hold positions. They converse and strategize. It is not a battle they plan to fight nor a war they wish to start. It will be a complete conquering requiring a smooth sweep.

Such things are not decided upon quickly. Every angle is inspected thoroughly and repeatedly. This takes skill and strategy. The aim is to hold awareness of the whole. Forward movement of this kind should be slow.

There are targets to decide. Which ones hide and which ones are irrelevant? In this battle the score is the core. Straight in. No diversion. Precise decision. Implosion.

This life has taught me to toe the line resiliently, surrendering to time, because incidents emerge with a mind of their own.

Sturdy, I row the rapid patterns of the foreword movement. I stay in tune with each separate quest. Observe. Steady. Do the work that leans against the thick breath of the herd.

We are divergent and ominous. Everything formed in us is powered by a self-love so infinite that it becomes a hurricane of pounding rain.

Vennie Kocsis

Wait and wonder is a skill that works in sync with timing. When the unknown is contained, let it view itself free. Then enact the deeds piece by piece, strategically.

The way of the warrior sees all. It holds integrity and passion. It surveys the landscape quietly, momentarily, while dancing still in movement.

Invisible, the warrior slides into position, hidden, and becomes all of what is to come. They each arrive alone.

Gathering, we become the storm.

Keeper of Backwards Men

I stand in this truth valiantly. I am unaffected by the injections of toxins from unhealed souls who throw their wounds at the world like swords. I will move forward no matter what because I have the guts and the resilience to take the blows.

Vennie Kocsis

I listen to hear and reply to share comradely passage
of the past when we understood grief.

Hard to believe what we survived. Here alive, we fight
for generational trauma breaking to relieve the aching.

Leave the ashes to become dust in the burned-up sun.
Used up children are now grownups coming undone.

Keeper of Backwards Men

There are no tears here. I do not cry. I keep my eyes sharply observing the other side. Any attempt at manipulation is thwarted by my intervention.

She sat in the car today. We talked telepathic. We came to an agreement. She wrote it all down.

I do protection. I am a mind mercenary. I enact what I must. I rise at dusk and watch till dawn. I'm a keeper of the caves holding the pirates at bay.

I drift past the scenes, observing, reading, and absorbing. I morph through days and ages, minutes moving too fast, hours passing too slowly. I see into hearts. So much shattered glass. So many missing pieces to recreate the puzzles. They wonder why we feel tired in the brain. It is the strain from the pain that remains.

Keeper of Backwards Men

We look at one another, and realization settles into our eyes. It's just us against this waning world.

The cusp of the feeling is real. We follow our own souls, walking this path alone

Vennie Kocsis

I have words to keep me warm, paintbrushes to pass the hours, sleep to block the memories, and those who live inside urging me through.

Battles fought alone leave blood drips. I crawl in caves to rest, let the wounds heal, and let the energy refresh before I restart this.

Don't live in dreams of a reality made from holograms flipped inside out. This is not the right path for the mission. Abort. Return to the portal.

Vennie Kocsis

It's deeper than the seas, but you humans, you fight over the most ridiculous things, problems with easy fixes.

Your psychodramas outweigh the effect of the traumas you leave behind in all the shattered and scattered minds.

Bring it down.

Demolition. We call action. We are not children of desire. We are born of fire.

Burn it down.

Keeper of Backwards Men

In the end, all she wanted was her own piece of heaven where her chest didn't feel heavy, smiles felt real, and she could be free, away from the ache left from picking up shards of her beautiful heart.

Vennie Kocsis

Patience short, I dismantle and abort. The light whispers. I answer with songs and verses. The darkness shrinks into shadows, a deliberate glimmer in hazy lights.

On this night I have cleansed again.

I am not the keeper of backwards men.

ABOUT THE AUTHOR

Vennie Kocsis is the author of "Cult Child," a memoir detailing her life growing up in an apocalyptic cult. She published her first book of poetry, "Dusted Shelves," in 2011. Her mindfulness journal, "Becoming Gratitude," inspires thankfulness and self-care.

Vennie promotes healing through writing and art. She is a strong advocate of mental health and increasing the protection of children.

To learn more visit: VennieKocsis.com

Vennie Kocsis